's to h

Text by David Bennett, Illustrations by Rosalinda Kightley
Series consultant Dr. John Becklake, Science Museum, London, England.
Educational consultant Barbara Cork.

All rights reserved.
Copyright ©1989 by Victoria House Publishing Ltd.
Bear Facts Series title, logo, and text ©1988 David Bennett.

Published in Great Britain in 1989 by
Marvel Books,
Arundel House, 13-15 Arundel Street, London WC2R 3DX.
Printed in the United Kingdom.
ISBN 1-85400-034-9

# Air

Words by David Bennett
Pictures by Rosalinda Kightley

The earth is wrapped in a blanket of air
called the atmosphere. You cannot see or
smell the air, but it is all around us.

Out in space there is no air, so an astronaut has to carry air in a backpack.

Air is important to all of us. We have to breathe air to stay alive.

Breathe in . . . and breathe out — you can feel the air moving through your body.

All living things need air — from little ants
to big farm animals.

Plants need air just like you do.
They take in air through tiny holes
in their leaves.

There is air in water, too. But you cannot breathe underwater. You would have to carry air in a special tank.

Some plants and animals can only live and breathe underwater. Fish take in air from the water through gills.

When air gets warm, it rises.
As warm air moves up, cooler air
rushes in to take its place. When this air gets
warm and rises, more cool air rushes in.

This moving air is called wind.
You can't see the wind, but
you can feel it.

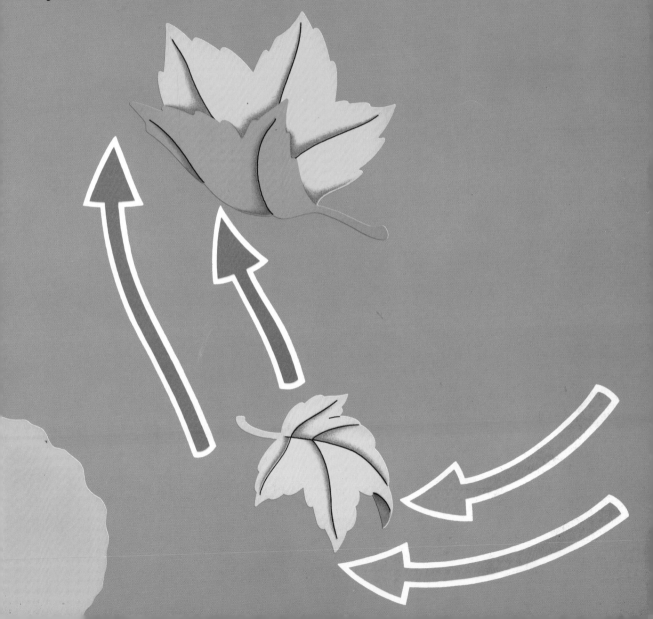

The wind blows clouds across the sky and makes trees sway in the breeze.

Wind blows all around the world.
The same wind that ruffles your hair
may have ruffled the fur on a polar bear
in the arctic.

A large balloon filled with warm air
will rise into the sky. The wind will push
the balloon along.

With a parachute, you can float down
to the ground. Air gets trapped under the
parachute and stops it from falling too fast.

The wind blows some kinds of plant seeds
from place to place.
Dandelion seeds have tiny parachutes to
help them float on the wind.

If they land on good soil, these seeds
may take root and grow into new plants.

The wind helps us in many ways.
It can turn the sails on a windmill
round and round.

It can push boats through the water.
It can dry laundry hanging on a line.

Sometimes the wind brings great storm clouds. A strong wind can blow so hard that it knocks down fences and trees.

A fire warms the house when it is cold and windy outside.
A fire will not burn without air.

When warm air rises inside your home,
cold air is sucked in around the doors and windows.

You might feel this cold air around
your feet. This is called a draught.

We need air all the time. It keeps us alive.
We breathe air in, and we breathe air out –
even while we sleep.

# BEAR REVIEW

1. The earth is wrapped in a blanket of air called the atmosphere.

2. All living things need air to stay alive.

3. Moving air is called wind.

4. We breathe air even while we sleep.